JOURNEY
THROUGH *Life*

WITH HEART,
SOUL & SPIRIT

Maddie,
May you be ever blessed
with inspiration that will
stir hearts.

Blessings
Jason Knox

POETRY BY
JASON P. KNOX

JOURNEY THROUGH LIFE WITH HEART,
SOUL & SPIRIT
Copyright ©2009 Jason P. Knox

ISBN-13: 978-1-926676-29-6

Printed by Word Alive Press

WORD ALIVE PRESS
Just Write!

131 Cordite Road, Winnipeg, Manitoba, R3W 1S1
www.wordalivepress.ca

Dedication

This collection of poems is from a wide span of my life. They are words from my heart trying to express what is within. This book is for anyone who needs to be encouraged and inspired. Some of the poems were specifically written with that in mind, for specific people that have crossed my path.

Although I could come up with many names, there are some specific people that I would like to make a special note of. The first is my Dad. He was a great blessing to me and was a great first glimpse of who Father God is. Mom, though at times I think we drive each other crazy, I have deeply appreciated your investment into my life for you are a major part of who I am today. Then there is Mr. Bob Duggan, my principal and teacher many, many years ago at Orangeville Christian School. I have to credit you for giving me an appreciation for writing by the encouragement you gave for me through my compositions.

Finally, the friends I made during my time at the Isaiah 61 winter school of '09 at Singing Waters Ministries. I know I blessed some of you with my poetic words, but at the same time many of you blessed and inspired me. Thanx.

This I Will Defend

I am a highland warrior,
Born to serve the high chieftain Lord.
Ruler of all Caledonia,
This I will defend.

So sound the uileann and bodhran,
Wake the fog of the early dawn,
Crowning all of Caledonia.

The war cry goes o'er loch and land,
Born to live for the final stand.
Motto of the MacFarlane's,
This I will defend.

Blue paint on the face,
The tartan in place.
Sword in the right hand,
Here we'll make our stand.
We declare to foe and friend,
This we will defend.

The Crushed Rose

A black rose blooming in the sun,
Love reaching is how it had begun.
Pricking Yourself on my thorn,
And new life was then born.

With Your blood I'm crimson white.

Delicate petals that You crush,
To release the perfume in a rush.
Gently pressed by design,
My beauty to last all time.

And with Your blood I'm crimson white,
The crushed rose in Your book of life.

One of my personal, favourite poems. I guess this comes from the core of my heart. A comfort in some ways in its inert poetic styling and yet it says so much. I've had varying responses from this poem, from awe that I was its composer to critics pointing out that crimson is a shade of red and so how can there be a crimson white. Yet if one were to think about it, it's by His crimson blood that our sins are made as white as snow, ergo crimson white.

Psalm 148

(Jason's translation)

Praise the Lord from the heavens above,
Praise Him, angels and heavenly hosts.
Sun, moon, and stars praise Him for His great love.
Praise Him in the highest heavens,
Let them praise from outer space,
For He set them into place.

Everything praise Him that is from this earth,
All great creatures of the deep blue sea,
Because He is the founder of their birth.
Lightning, thunder and all weather,
All natural forces around,
Let your praises be heaven bound.

Let the mountains and hills break forth with song,
Shrubs and grasses of the field sing out,
Praise the Lord all trees that are tall and strong.
All creatures great and small praise Him,
Birds of the air take flight and sing,
For Jesus has given you wings.

Kings of the earth and leaders of nations,
You princes and all rulers of earth,
Praise Him for what He's done in creation.
All young men and their fair maidens,
Old men and children in the street,
Praise the Lord and get to your feet.

Let all creation praise His holy name,
His glory fills all of the heavens,
Praise Him and you will never be the same.
He shall raise us up as great kings,
The Lord rules from shore to shore,
Everything just praise the Lord.

Psalm From the Heart

All praise to the great Jehovah,
With Whom all things and nothing rhyme.
The one Alpha and Omega,
Eternal both within and out of time.

You, Lord are the one true Word,
Yet no words can fully explain You.
The source of all life and all breathe,
And yet so many would choose death.

You sacrifice all deity,
For the mere chance to love me.
Oh, the words spinning in my head,
My God! You saved me from the dead.

Selah!

Psalm of Pondering

Flowing like a river from the throne,
Flowing out unto all of His own,
Father's love comes as a holy rain.

Are there more words that I can write?
To describe my spiritual sight,
What I sense is enough to fry my brain.

Paper and pens will soon all run out,
But it's all God, there is no doubt,
Wisdom is at a loss with it all.

The delights of earth could not compare,
To what the Father wants to share,
Oh, how our vision is so very small.

Art Worship

Storyteller speak to me a tale,
Tell of the Word that will not fail.
Paint a picture within my mind,
That goes well beyond all time.

Oh weaver of words do now speak,
For it is the simple Truth that I seek.
Bind my broken heart with romance,
Of the King and His bride as they dance.

And minstrel let your fingers now move,
To strike all the chords that will soothe.
Write a song that would be for the One,
The Father, Holy Spirit and the Son.

All artists now express your heart,
Praising the Creator with your art.
Be it pencil, music, stone or paint,
Praise Him each and every saint.

Love is our purpose so divine,
To be what He sees us as before time.
As His own very best friend,
Beyond all that we can imagine.

Allegory

Caldorian minstrels play on their harps of gold,
Listen and hear their ancient story unfold.
Of a land and of a time forgotten,
It's of a prince child that was begotten.

Symballens pound on drums their tale to add,
Within it the heart beats of that prince's dad.
The trial and tests that they went through,
The fullness of it only an angelic host knew.

Blastells now join with their trumpets of brass,
It's all a love tale that will never pass.
As it is a truth that resounds in all,
True love was nearly sealed behind a wall.

Galidorun the once long forgotten land,
Becomes the focus of each and all man.
The final battle lines were drawn out,
Where the prince wins with a greater shout.

Brass Snake

Crafty as a serpent, yet as a pure dove,
The price and cost to express My love.
To undo the lie of an age old snake,
My sacrifice is what it must take.

The brass of judgement raised on high,
Yet your freedom it now draws nigh.
A rugged pole on a lonely hill,
Not mine, but it's the Father's will.

I am the brass snake that's to save you,
Lift your eyes unto Me is all you need do.
Yet upon that pole I did not stay,
For My triumph came on the third day.

Israel once made the same mistake,
For an image, Myself, they did forsake.
Tell Me how to get it across,
Beloved I Am no longer on that cross.

This by no means is an attack against any particular denomination within the Body of Christ. The imagery of the crucifix hinted in this poem could be almost anything within the Body that has had a holy use, but inadvertently becomes pretty much an image of worship. A curse from the fall perhaps that leaves us needing something physical for our eyes to fix upon for security within our belief. We all need to look more with the eyes of our heart and fix our course upon what our inward eyes see Christ doing.

Illusion Revealed

With beauty, hard to describe,
You draw from nation and tribe.
They gather in awe before your throne,
Oh, how your kingdom has so grown,
From simple seeds that were sown.

Your wisdom, so great indeed,
Angel and man take your lead.
As creation falls before your feet,
Seems there's not one you can't beat,
No time that you'd ever call retreat.

You calculate, each move,
Yet you've nothing to prove.
Your greatness, you've nothing to hide,
Yet a misstep in your stride,
You see, I know about the pride.

The truth is, I can see your lie,
I know the true One whom you defy.
The made isn't greater than the Maker,
You have become a petty faker,
A jealous, greedy taker.

Time's coming, the end's within sight,
The Lamb has quite a lion's bite!
And all the truth will then be known,
Before the rightful King's throne,
Your place of honour now blown.

Ecc. 7:1-4

Sadness can be good for the heart,
Healing with tears in every part.
Sorrow over laughing to bring peace,
To allow His Kingdom to increase.

Chorus:

Oh Lord, why does there have to be pain,
With love falling like the rain.
Oh Lord, what is the true worth,
With pain beginning at birth.
Why does there have to be pain,
When love falls like rain.

Mourning seems to live with the wise,
Breaking the bands love always ties.
Grieving over praising to heal wounds,
A wander in the hot sandy dunes.

Chorus:

Praising needs to break this old curse,
Before the pain can become worse.
Precious Jesus enter in and heal,
A desire for a peace that's so real.

Valley of Bones

Gathering sand and twirling dust,
Heaping of ash and piling rust.
Dead calm on this wadi plain,
Lifelessly waiting for the rain.

Gloomering clouds and greying sky,
Rumours come that more will yet die.
Chalk dry cracks grow wide to devour,
Questions birth, is this the final hour?

Then thunder breaks with lightning flash,
Echoes of an ancient fight's clash.
The shadows dance thru skull and bone,
Only jackal and raven call this home.

Surprise comes with changing winds,
Blessings falls as the rain begins.
The whispered words from an age before,
Unlock the bars of death's door.

Sinews rise, muscles reform and skin enwraps,
The armour shines.
While banners and capes flap free of ragged scraps,
The order defines.
Bodies form, units appear and order comes,
With weapons full.
While living and breath come thru the pierced Son,
The army of Joel.

Valley of bones this is no more,
Ranking man and horse of war.
His peace will be made by sworded hand,
The world succumbs to the Son of Man.

By the Artist's Hand

Dust covered scrap of linen,
Torn, tattered and given in,
To lies told and love forsaken.

Dull coloured piece of nothing,
You know there's got to be something,
So tired of trying, tired of looking.

Birth given some artwork of heaven,
Yet needing to taste the forgiven,
To find a higher way of livin'.

Then the Artist found that bit of linen,

Dust removed, the prize to reveal,
Mends, repairs add to its appeal,
To love that will never conceal.

Bold colours that could not shine less,
A piece of art that surely is priceless,
So free of trying, no longer hopeless.

Signed by the Master's own hand,
A sight to behold by all man,
Revived art by the Son of Man.

Praise the Artist for the work He has done!

Colours

Red, the blood, from Jesus' forehead,
As He prayed in the garden,
Needing strength for what was to come,
The beating for our sin.

Colours, a rainbow shattered,
Colours flowing for three days,
As we were set free.

Purple, the curtain in the temple,
Ripped to open the way for us,
Black, no colour, the ninth hour,
Jesus is filled with sin.

Colours, a rainbow shattered,
Colours flowing for three days,
As we were set free.

White, the lily beside the tomb,
Witness to Jesus risen undefeated,
Cleansed of all dark sin,
Jesus freed us with colours.

All Hail

All hail to the reigning King,
Come now lift up a voice and sing,
To you warrior of noble birth,
Offer up all that you are worth,
Your sword, your shield, your defense,
Submit all within the King's presence.

All hail to the ruling King,
Come now lift up a voice and sing,
To you oh daughter of Zion,
Bow before this unsafe Lion,
Your poise, your grace, your beauty,
Present all as your royal duty.

All hail to the highest King,
Listen now as all creation will sing,
From vale to mountain peak,
Hear the words nature would speak,
All life, all light, all in all,
Before the High King, bow and fall.

All hail the eternal King,
Angels of the unseen must sing,
Hell's depths to heaven's heights,
From the dark's darkest to the light,
Angels that fly, that crawl,
Worship Him the King above all!

Dance

Dance before the Messiah,
Dance before the King,
Dance now, don't hesitate a thing.

Dance for our precious Lord,
Dance now in one accord,
For He has set us free!

Dance before the Messiah,
Dance before our King,
Dance now, don't be afraid to sing.

Dance for our precious One,
Dance now for what He has done,
Plunge into His love sea!

Now dance, ah ya, dance,
Dance, dance for our King!

Hallelujah!

Wonder

As the ocean waves roll,
And the eagle soars on high,
I'm amazed and left to wonder why,

As the sun now sets,
And the colours dance the sky,
I surrender that I can't deny,

Your beauty surrounds,
Your glory abounds,
A genius of creative design.

Thank You Lord for this day and this time.

Another

Another poem has come to birth,
Another verse upon the paper,
With delight the pen will dance,
With passion it will write,

Another prose of simplicity,
Another ode of nobility,
As liquid voice the ink flows,
As streams of frozen display,

Inspiration will remain,
As long as You are King.

Darling Child

Lullaby and goodnight,
To your dreams hold on tight,
Lullaby and goodnight,
Let your dreams be outta sight.

Rock and roll, soothe your soul,
Let God take control,
No more nightmares to dream,
No more monsters to make you scream.

So goodnight darling child,
Till the night is through,
Oh, goodnight my darling child,
Till the day is new.

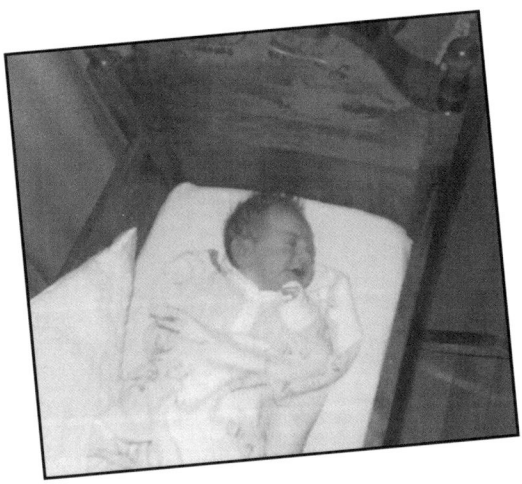

Love

Want to feel the power of love, just say His name.
Say His name, and you'll never be the same.

Jesus, King of kings,
Jesus, Lord of lords.

Want to see the nations roll like the ocean's tide.
Saddle up with Him, saddle up for the ride.

He is there on His steed,
See His pennants fly so high.

Want to hear the Father's loving voice.
His voice, just listen, it's the simplest choice.

Abba, my Father,
Abba, my Daddy.

Father

A rushing of wings,
A single voice sings,
Moving the heart strings.

Father Your voice,
My choice.

A single desire,
A goal to aspire,
Seeking to acquire.

Father Your way,
This day.

A passion of heart,
Oh, never depart,
Where do we start.

Father Your love,
My love.

My prayer Father is for Your love to consume all that is
me.
My desire is to have You as my desire, my passion, forever.
Let the concerns of everything vanish so that You are all
that I see.
Amen.

Father's Lap

And when it all comes down to it,
Hear Father say, "Come and just sit,"
There is room, oh so much room,
There is room in His lap to spare.

Hear the love in His voice as He calls,
In their own words He speaks to all,
There is love, oh so much love,
A love that knows only increase.

Feel the arms of love reach for you,
Just receive is all you need do,
The blessing, so much blessing,
It's the blessing of our Father.

Look deep into your very heart,
Only a mere crack for healing to start,
The fullness, oh the fullness,
To begin to know His fullness.

And that is where it all comes down to,
Just two, the Father and you,
There is room, oh so much room,
There is room in His lap to spare.

The Drop

On the cusp, at the very edge,
Where something small turns to something great.
To hold on, grasping the ledge,
Hold on to your breathe, not too much longer to wait!

With a sigh, a pleasant gasp,
To plunge and dive, it comes after so long and last.
A time to turn, a season of change,
Reward for the few that held on so long and fast.

Thrill of risk, the wilds of the unknown,
But oh for the delights as we now see we've grown!

Taking the Father's hand and we shall change,
To become alike with the Son of Man.

High Freedom Psalm

Mountains high and through valleys low,
Father I'll go wherever You will go.
Through the floods and the fire,
You remain my heart's desire.

With hinds feet I will climb the heights,
Eager to share upon all Your delights.
Noble strength You've bestowed to me,
My spirit is so alive and so free.

Uncontainable joy is mine,
As I am with You there is no time.
Swept along with Your compassion and grace,
Still I hunger to see You face to face.

And from the river bank I will arise,
Like on eagle's wings I take to the skies.
My lips bear the sweetness of freedom's kiss,
A mere sample of Your eternal bliss.

Bigger Wholly God

Thoughts and plots play in my mind,
It makes me think it's 'bout time,
Dreams and plans bloom before me,
It just takes my breath away.

Bigger, so much bigger than can be imagined,
What can I do?
What can I say?
Cause it's purely God,
Wholly God.

Pen and pad demand the words,
To tell of what's deep inside,
Noun and verb try to bear it,
To grasp what I just cannot.

Bigger, so much bigger than can be imagined,
Not by my hand,
Not by my will,
Cause it's purely God,
Wholly God.

Sun and moon cannot fathom,
As I am awed by it all,
Day and night have not the strength,
As I see it all unfold.

Bigger, so much bigger than can be imagined,
What more to say?
What more to write?
Cause it's purely God,
Wholly God.

Free Falling

And now I'm free falling,
Free falling into You,
I open my arms,
Outstretched in surrender,
And just let myself free fall.

Like a leaf that's surrendered,
Has given up its life,
I fall from my security,
To be carried upon the breeze of Your breathe.

And as I'm free falling,
Free falling without a care,
I open my heart,
Overwhelmed by wonder,
That all it took was a free fall.

Oh God catch me up in Your wonder,
The awesomeness,
The glory,
Let me free fall into You.

It's Not Right

There's a void in my heart, but not my soul,
I've been made complete, yet am not whole.
It's not right for a man to be alone.

I am filled with joy, but lone in grief,
With the riches of a king, victim of a thief.
It's not right for a man to be alone.

There's yet a whole to be found,
When love will resound,
No longer will I be alone.

I am a son of Adam, but where's my Eve,
Many blessings given, less one receive,
It's not right for a man to be alone.

Many dreams I have, but none to share,
God You are so just, yet it seems unfair,
It's not right for a man to be alone.

There's yet two to become one,
Then this poem will be done,
No longer will I be alone.

Romance

The yearning of the heart,
That is where one must start,
It is a mystery words lack,

The muscle behind love,
Its ways so few can know of,
Yet there lies the despair within,

When romance is denied its sway.

The beating of my heart,
Its set for one apart,
That girl in mystery's shadow,

The music is pushing on,
It keeps me awake till dawn,
Yet there lies the despair within,

When romance is unknown today.

And now for the question of all,
Please someone answer the call,
All I ask, is to know where to start,
When I wish to win a lady's heart.

Let Us Celebrate

This day, the mirror of what's to come,
A bride and a groom will unite as one.
The covenant of both hope and love,
The foretaste from the kingdom above.

Let us celebrate and let us rejoice.

Today, the union of two hearts,
Take a brave step toward a new start.
The excitement of a future bright,
The promise of a life of delight.

Let us celebrate and let us rejoice.

What the Father brings together,
Let no one ever tear asunder.
The preview to the fullness of His plan,
When we the bride wed the Son of Man.

So, let us celebrate and let us rejoice!

Betrothal

Scent of phlox and lilac fill the room,
The expectation of something soon.
Do I dare to investigate?
Or shall I pray and simply wait.

Sound of an unknown song fills the air,
It's wafting is neither here nor there.
The words I can't decipher,
But it would seem more like laughter.

I see rainbow light like from prism glass,
The covenant will ever last.
A truth that seems very strange,
Faithfulness that will never change.

Now comes a sense of a gentle touch,
A caress that means and says so much.
It's almost too much to believe,
And all I need do is just receive.

Out of puzzlement there now comes the scene,
A betrothal that has so long been.
The groom that's awaiting His bride,
And here it is all up to me to decide.

Step in eternal life like it's a dance,
Eyes on Him; there's no hesitance.
Sense of touch, sight, smell and sound,
Forever will now be unbound.

Ode to My Lover

To walk through the mirror glass,
To be with You, my Love, at last,
As crystal light dances before my eyes,
And eternal timelessness sheds the disguise,
I see throne room and glass sea.

To hear what is beyond sound,
To be with You, my Love, unbound,
As angels fall prostrate to You, oh King,
And welcome me as I come and kiss Your ring,
I will know love and be free.

To feel what is truly real,
To be free of this world conceal,
The heaven's paths lying before me run,
An adventure at each turn with the Son,
I will run and not grow faint.

To smell the ethereal air,
To be free and be without a care,
The woodlands breathe my true Love's name,
A romance from which I'll ne'er be the same,
And I'll see each friend a saint.

To faith that first stepping dare,
To be with You, my Lover, not a care,
This dreamlike ode becomes what is true,
And surrender is all I need to do,
I am Yours, Lord, and You are mine.

If I Had One Wish

If I had one wish, it would be to know you,
To hold you till the sky was no longer blue
If I had one wish, it would be to love you,
To love you through and through.
If I had one wish, one wish to be with you.

The Bride

On a fiery horse she rides,
Only one man may take her,
A Kingly groom in whom she confides.

With her armor, yet a white dress,
Only one understands her,
A Kingly knight she longs to caress.

Her hair flying with freedom,
Only the truest One knows her,
Side by side they reveal His kingdom.

She is many, yet she is one,
Only His Spirit will unite her,
As the Groom says the I do's are done.

We Are the Bride... Resistance Is Futile

Composed from race upon race,
Uniqueness blend into one face.

A collective with one mind,
Sought perfection will come in time.

We are the Bride... resistance is futile,
As in the end all will bow.

Fourteen hundred miles cubed,
All creation will be subdued.

Both sexes knit together in one,
The virgin Bride of the holy son.

We are the bride... resistance is futile,
As in the end all will bow...

To our Groom.

The Sword of Love

He did not come to bring us peace,
Yet each day His Kingdom sees increase.
He brought a sword to the fight,
That has quite a unique bite.
It's called love, a sword of love.

Chorus:
In a world where there's hate,
There's a better path to take,
Fight back with love.
In a world of endless night,
Fight back with love's pure light,
The sword of love.

Peace is so hard to reach out for,
We will not see relief from this war.
So Christ brought us this one tool,
Strange it seems to any fool.
Like a dove, a sword of love.

Chorus:

Bridge:
Like a flame to gas,
It has quite a blast.
Let it hit your heart,
Consume every part.
It divides spirit and soul,

In order to make whole.
The sword of love.

He puts the sword into our hand,
He now has us under His command.
Go to the night with this flame,
And this war won't be the same.
With this sword of love, His sword of love.

"Do not suppose that I have come to bring peace to the earth. I did not come to bring peace, but a sword." Matt. 10:34

And now these three remain: faith, hope and love. But the greatest of these is love. I Cor. 13:13

Stand

Oh Watcher, there upon the wall,
What does your gaze see?
The city hangs upon your call,
Words of assurity.

Oh Sentinel, think Elisha,
Those with us are more.
Our King, Lion of Judah,
The foe all abhor.

Stand your ground now for His Bride,
Don't ever look to the aside.
Stand with the boldness of a lion,
For lo, your King is of Mount Zion.
Stand your ground, wait His return,
In your heart, feel His passion burn.

Oh Sentry, keep the night lights lit,
Nightmares want to rise.
This is not the time to quit,
His eagle rules the skies.

Oh Lookout, you are not alone,
More towers stand strong.
Though posted high on your own,
You are where you belong.

Stand your ground before the foe,

You do more than you know.
Stand with the boldness of a lion,
For lo, your King is of Mount Zion.
Stand as your post does bring peace,
The citizen's gaze on you won't cease.

Oh Watcher, there upon the wall,
What does Your heart see?

On the Cusp

On the cusp, on the edge,
The cliff face is just ahead,
Change is coming here soon,
Be it the morrow or this noon.

Stay the course, we near the verge,
It's just around the curve,
Feel the changing of wind,
No surrender, don't give in.

The cup of time reaches the brim,
It's your choice to sink or swim,
Stand your ground without chance,
No time for hesitance.

On the cusp, on the edge,
Don't fear the drop of the ledge,
Those wings are meant to fly,
You see, the limit is no longer the sky.

Preparation

Father, I feel a rush, a move in the spirit winds.
A desire from deep within the wells of passion and hope.
A dream yet in the foggy shadows of the yet to come.

What is it that is beyond the grasp of now?
What is the phantom that easily evades the fingers of
thought?

I know there's something there, I can feel it,
A shift in shadows, a pause in the breeze, a ringlet in
the waters.

It's like a yet achieved triumphant, a taste of a victory in
the foreseeable future.

Father prepare me so I may receive the reality of this
destine thing.
I want to be ready to embrace it with the warmth that I
am not yet aware that it deserves.

Prepare me, Lord.

Promise Land Map

Drawn to the black light,
Like a moth to the flame,
With the shadow's trick,
Nothing remains the same.

Do I need this greyness,
Like a sunflower night,
Drive the blanket fog,
Restoring truth to my sight.

As blind will lead blind,
I grasp for just one hand,
The map is lost to me,
Lord take me to the Promised Land.

Restless

Like a horse chomping at the bit,
Restless,
Like a child being told to just sit,
Restless,

Restless, oh I am so restless,
Tired of the same old circumstance,
It's time to step out and take a chance.
Restless, oh I am so restless,
Doing the same once again is insane,
As this old horse wants to shake its mane.

Like an ocean inching up the shore,
Restless,
Like a knight longing to go to war,
Restless,

Restless, oh I am so restless,
Come on let's rise up and let's take some land,
It's time to rise up and simply make a stand.
Restless, oh I am so restless,
Getting tired of this scene of desert sand,
Can't take going round this mount again!

With a roar, shaking off this old chain,
Restless,
In this place I no longer will remain,
Restless.
I want to move forward to see,
Restless,
I want to move till the Lord makes me...

Breathless.

Risk Taker

Oh, risk taker is what I long to be,
His-story maker I so long to be,
But it's that risk that troubles me.

To step out of my comfort zone,
To walk into what to me is the unknown,
Release my claim to all that I would own.

Oh, risk taker it roars within my heart,
It threatens to tear me all apart,
But still I ask where do I start.

To step off and take that one plunge,
There's the edge, the urge I feel to lunge,
A war of thoughts of cost for that plunge.

Father, I know You will be there for me,
But now dare I ask that You would push me,
Let the risk taker become set free.

Oh God, I want to do the insane,
Break free from this world's mundane,
And grab ahold of the Lion's mane.

Ruach, blow me from this cliff face,
For within You risk has not a trace.

Soar

The prowling wolves are now the prey,
As they face the Lion, Ancient of Days.
And don't fret o'er the things of night,
As you're watched by the King of light.

Take His hand and He will lead you,
On paths trod by only the few.
Thru forest glen and meadows green,
Marvel at sites ne'er before seen.

Davidic words beat within your heart,
Flowing o'er your lips as you impart.
An outflow from the Father above,
Words of grace, mercy and unending love.

You desire to go on ever higher,
You long for the Consuming Fire.
To see the golden streets and crystal sea,
And soar like the eagle high and free.

Let the holy winds lead as they blow,
Dance and flit as the Spirit would go.
Forget the eyes and thoughts of mere man,
You walk a higher purpose and plan.

So soar eagle, soar high and clear,
Soar young eagle without fear,
Soar.

Artwork by Caroline Wood

A Sergeant's Entry

As the final pages unfold,
The rise will increase,
The spirit war as been foretold.

On the global chess board played,
Pity the ignorant soul,
Not one is free from the tirade.

All must have their senses forebear,
The passive will perish,
Can't deny there is this warfare.

Look there, the One who is in control,
The Lamb is a Lion,
The Sovereign who's never lost His rule.

As the story draws to a close,
The start will begin,
The Omega ends it for His foes.

As for me, I await the change,
My next role to be played,
I await for the pieces to rearrange.

Ready to serve, where deployed.

Battle Psalm

There's a flag flapping in the wind,
I hear the high trumpet call.
Birds of prey gathering above,
They beckon to one and to all.

There's a lull rolling 'cross the field,
Before the rhythmic hoof beat.
Surreal mist lingers like ghosts,
It waits for the foes to meet.

There's a taste rising too few know,
The foretaste of what's to come.
No escape it's been foretold,
A sequence to the final sum.

There's now a rumble do you feel?
As two armies cross the ground.
You'll have to decide on a side,
No neutral place is to be found.

There's no doubt as to the outcome,
Odds of favour to one side.
See their general sitting on His horse,
He alone will beat the foe tide.

They will charge and they will fall,
See in the end who stands up tall,
Jesus Christ, Lord Ruler of all,
Jesus Christ, Lord Ruler of all.

Sword of the Spirit
painting by Craig Wood

War & Peace

The sword's edge welcomes the dawn,
Its music is heard as it is drawn,
The light's first rays kiss its blade,
The crimson there you can't evade.

In the midst of this peace, peace,
The war is on the increase,
The Prince of Peace has come and gone,
The Lion of Judah rose on that dawn.

Yes the gentle Lamb had His day,
Now watch the Lion have His way,
That's not just the sound of war,
That my friend is His rumbling roar.

You can either kneel or stand,
But sitting there is not the plan,
To be in the world and not of it,
And yet there you all just still sit.

Rise up you mighty men of war,
To take this land from shore to shore,
The way of peace has come and gone,
It was a Lion that rose on that dawn.

We battle not with flesh and blood,
Yet I won't be taken by the flood,
So with my sword in hand I stand,
I will fight to take the promise land.

See the east and that silvery light,
It's a sword that will slay the night,
There will be a victor's crown to fit,
But not given to those who just sit.

So will you follow and obey,
Or give in to religious sway,
Get a spine, stand for the Son of Man,
It's by His strength alone you can.

The razor edge isn't yours to fear,
Across the enemy's back to sear,
Saddle your horse and warrior ride,
See the change in the war's tide.

The Lion of Judah has a roar,
He has already won this war,
He has defeated the ugly horde,
And peace will come by His sword.

Warrior's Creed

O Lord let the warrior arise,
Arise within me,
O Lord let the warrior arise,
Stand before the enemy.

With feet shod with Your peace,
A gospel that will never cease,
Let the warrior arise, arise within me.

With Your truth belted at my waist,
The enemy we will give to chase,
Let the warrior arise, arise within me.

My chest shielded by Your purity,
The victory is an assurity,
Let the warrior arise, arise within me.

With Your word, a cleaving sword,
I will face the massing horde,
Let the warrior arise, arise within me.

With faith as my reliant shield,
To You alone, Lord may I yield,
Let the warrior arise, arise within me.

A helmet of only Your saving grace,
My strength to the end of this race,
Let the warrior arise, arise within me.

One thing to add to this for all my days,
My shoulders caped with Your praise,
Let the warrior arise, arise within me.

O Lion of Judah, Ancient of Days,
Let this warrior arise, arise on this day.

Duty Calls

Here they come upon the sandy shore,
Blasts and gun shots fight the ocean's roar.
They come united with their cause,
To oppose the breakers of moral laws.

If it were any other kind of time,
A sun chair with an iced key lime.
To just watch the birds dive and play,
Just a pleasant old kind of beach day.

Yet another mortar blast,
And those thoughts cannot last,
As duty calls them further up and in.

As they charge the enemy's line,
How many spirits leave their shell behind?
A broken body fallen on reddish sand,
Never to walk again, let alone stand.

They are so young and seem so brave,
Yet how many fall in an unmarked grave?
One blast will kill, one will bury,
This war scene beyond what is scary.

Yet at the eleventh hour, month and day,
We will remember the cost and the pay,
As duty calls them further up and in.

Loyal to the Call

Sacrifice of self for something that is higher,
Questioning of each step and every desire.

Does this lead forward or off the side?
Another fork and time again you have to decide.

Who, what, where and when lines with His heart for
you,
So many may be called, yet in the end there are so few.

Yes at times we want to forget it,
Too hard to bear, the price,
So tired of self sacrifice!
What about me and my heart?
Don't I have a say to my part?
Yes, at times, damn well forget it!

Insanity comes again as we come delusional,
Once more we choose to be loyal to the call.

Does this lead forward or off the side?
Another decision upon Yahweh I will confide.

Who, what, where and when lines with His heart for
you,
Determined now to the call, I will be one of those few!

Bitter Sweet Day

Bitter sweet was that day,
The day You tore open the way.
Outside Your Son died on a tree,
Meanwhile it opened, set us free.

Oh bitter sweet day.

Irony displayed on the earth,
To show all our value and worth.
Beyond all cost and beyond price,
It sacrificed Jesus Christ.

Oh irony display,
On that bitter sweet day.

Better still, the third day,
That day sealed open the way.
Inside now the Spirit can move,
The trials of life to soothe.

So better still,
The irony display,
Hence that bitter sweet day.

Coming yet, our King's return,

Oh, we Your bride so do yearn.
Beyond all dreams, hope and all thought,
When all things are as they ought.
And coming yet,
So much better still,
The ironic display,
Cause of love's bitter sweet day.

Easter's Ballad

The cross, the plus sign, exclamation mark,
The place death tried to kill the life spark.
The tomb, the grave, the cold stone and bowel of earth,
The place where a new race saw its birth.

As the sun rose and the moon found its rest,
Love overcame its greatest test.
That rolling stone set more in motion,
A rising tide greater than any ocean.

The cry, the yell that came and filled the sky,
The Victor rose to show death it could die.
The veil is torn; the way is now made open,
Our past debts can now be forgotten.

Cry

In quote of the band, The Choir,
Lyrics suited for this very hour.

"A sad face is good for the heart,
Go on cry it can be a cruel world,
A sad face is good for the heart of a girl."

I wish I could be there to shed tears too,
As one you love joins the chosen few.
It can hurt as they graduate,
To see them again will be a bit of a wait.

They have moved on to be with The One we love,
In heaven's splendid realm up and above.
Oh, the wonders they must now see,
The flowery meadows, the great crystal sea,
Most of all, the Lover of all, Who set them free.

So with mixed emotions we bid adieu,
There's sadness, happiness and maybe envy too,
For the veil for them is now lifted away,
Imagine the music that they can now play!
Yet here we are to say one last goodbye,
As we release them to the sweet by and by...

So go on it's okay for you to cry.

Heart Broken

I stand here with my broken heart,
Blood spattered torn apart,
My scream is lost in the howling wind.

I hear a voice, that echo is my own voice,
I'm feeling like there was no choice,
The demons taunt me with shards of a dream.

I can no longer stand with this weight,
No I can no longer stay and wait,
My death would be a welcomed robe.

Dreams passed down from above break,
Denied love is so hard for me to take,
All passion slogs through a quagmire.

Yet I will stand, wait here, storm or not,
Cause my Father is all I really got,
My cries, my pain I know He does hear.

I will not lie down and just die, Despair,
I will stand by His strength to bear,
Yes, this pain will yet see me grow.

I stand here with a broken heart,
Yet that is where it needs to start,
Father it all depends upon You.

In my school years, I met this guy. At first we really didn't like each other a single bit, but by the end of the school year we became close friends. He helped bring me out of my shell and I drew him in closer to the Lord. Though I never knew this until after high school, when he was sharing his testimony with some of our friends. He accredited to me and my life example for his being drawn to Jesus; it blew me away and humbled me. As a result he had set his course on being involved in ministry to share with others the true freedom he had found in the Lord because of his friend who wouldn't compromise his faith. We even bounced around ideas of going to YWAM together.

However, October 23, 1990 tragedy changed all our youthful dreams as a tragic construction accident at his job took my friend home. I still remember exactly what I was doing when I got the news, I was gardening. I immediately dropped what I was doing and went straight for my room, where I collapsed on my bed grieving. In the process of that grief I wrote the words of Tears of Pain, which really helped me walk out that process of mourning. I still miss him greatly, mind, but the grieving is over, now to look forward to our reunion.

Tears of Pain

Oh, I loved you more than a brother,
A friend so close, there was no other.
We both longed to serve the King,
But now I'm left to do our thing.
Your life was stolen from you,
And I don't know what to do.

Tears of pain fall from my eyes,
Tears of love pour from my heart
You were here, but now in the skies,
And with you went part of me.

Oh, you had a love no one could take,
Your strong will to serve no one could break.
We laughed and we cried as one,
But now an evil has been done.
Death came early to your soul,
Leaving your body so cold.

Tears of pain fall from my eyes,
Tears of love pour from my heart
You were here, but now in the skies,
And with you went part of me.

Oh, God why another friend so dear,
Your great plan is no longer so clear.
Yes, I know he's safe and warm,
But I am alone and so torn.
Peace to me You can't deny,
As in sorrow I now cry.

Encouragement

This poem is for the broken hearted,
For those grieving for the departed.
The cares of the world are not theirs,
But now belongs to the heirs.

This worded rhyme is hope for the morrow,
A lit path for ones lost in their sorrow.
The night will last for only a season,
Don't weary yourself to find the reason.

These heart thoughts written out for you to read,
There's a day from all grief we will be freed.
When He will wipe away every tear,
And the Lion will devour every fear.

Quiet

Sit and be quiet, be still,
Surrender of your will.
To hear the amazing sound,
Creation's song all around.

Sit and be quiet, one time,
Turn off your mind, it's no crime.
It to hear a still small voice,
The first step is your choice.

Sit and be quiet, right here,
There's nothing for you to fear.
His lap, an amazing place,
Listen, the heart beat of grace.

Sit and be quiet, be still.

Path of Courage

Hear the roar in the forest glen,
Go and be drawn within.
Your heart knows what you'll see,
Though your mind tells you to flee.

Now take a deep breath, swallow,
Listen by spirit and follow.
There is a path that lies there,
So you go without a care.

Walk under the protective shade,
Listen there's a brook in the glade.
In which the Lion, He awaits,
So dear one, do not hesitate.

At times you can run, at times no,
Either way hear your heart say go.
The trees are the hall for this King,
The birds, His angelic choir sing.

See the Lion King with flowing mane,
Doubts and fear no longer remain.
You see now you're more than princess,
With courage you are His lioness.

Lions

The toothless lion is on the prowl,
But you need not fear his growl.
For he has met his match.

With pride he roams round the forest glen,
Seeking the weak and forgotten.
For that's how he feels strong.

Now rise up and look there to the east,
Robed in light is the true King of each beast.
He wants you to join His royal pride,
He waits for you to match Him in stride.
Oh the patience of grace.

True faith needs to reside in your heart,
Or your fears will simply tear you apart.
Trust in the path even when it's unseen,
As it is a way in which He's already been.
Oh the assurance of hope.

The toothless lion is still out there,
But you need not fear his glare.
For you're a lioness of the Lord.

Assured you are part of the King's pride,
You don't have any need to hide.
Oh lioness of the Lion of Judah.

A project during the Isaiah 61 School was to make a painting, kind of a relying on the Spirit for inspiration. Then later we drew names from a bucket and the name we drew was the prophetic recipient of the paintwork we had done. Now during this school, there were two Asian women who kind of adopted me and became major encouragers in regards to my poetry. One of them was Vera, I had really blessed her with a poem that I felt the Father had me write for her and on occasion she would ask if I would do another one for her.

Well, it must have been the Father's will. At my turn to draw a name, I thought... "Oh no." This especially came to mind when one piece of paper literally would not let go of my hand, so I surrendered to the fact that it was the name I was to select and sure enough the name on that piece of paper was Vera. The first thing she says when she comes forward to accept my artwork was, "I want a poem to go with this."

Fortunately, Father was already on top of it because the phrases for the poem were already being choreographed in my mind. Even now when I think back on that, I cannot deny that the Holy Spirit was orchestrating the whole thing.

By Grace

Oh stalwart one mounted upon the shore,
Your roots go deep holding the Rock that is sure.
Through wind storms and crashing sea.
You hold fast for all to see.
By grace no leaf out of place.

Oh watcher you've remained upright and true,
And watch as each sunrise foretells the day is new.
You relish in ocean mist,
A reminder of Saviour's kiss.
By grace you will see His face.

Oh faithful one you ne'er fear the rising tide,
For you know well in whom you always confide.
You flower for Him alone,
The fragrance frames His throne.
By grace feel His loving embrace.

Oh ageless one holding the Rock so very tight,
Know that you are His greatest delight.
A refuge for His small ones,
When their world seems undone.
For by grace in you they see His face.

Transformation

In this wilderness land,
No water in the desert sand,
The shade comes from a lone rock stand.

The days are all so hot and long,
The night alone with cold so strong,
This site comes across as so wrong.

A subtle sway in the ways of grace,
It begins with the mere faintest trace,
There still is hope for this barren place.

It's a soft prayer raised to the skies,
A hint to the imprisoned cries,
Barred behind many years of lies.

Soon the answer comes with sweet rain,
That rock becomes pliable again,
With the release of hurt and pain.

In time a river begins to flow,
And the truth now starts to show,
That rock's a heart, don't you know!

The wilderness, now lush and green,
No more lonely desert can be seen,
In the presence of Father, this heart has been.

So let all the healing rains come,
Let the river be the downpour's sum,
And revel in the Father's Kingdom come.

Metamorphous Commission

Cleanse me in a blood shower,
Dress me up like a flower,
And plant me in Your table land.

Erase these images from my mind,
And make me a one of a kind,
Unique in You so will I stand.

Birth within me a new regime,
Plot out what is Your's to scheme,
The mystery gift that's for all man.

Tear down walls so I cannot hide,
Disperse from me all of my pride,
And mold me by Your sovereign hand.

Roll back the skies, roll back the skies,
I want to see into the spirit realm.
Roll back the skies, roll back the skies,
I want to know the reality realm.

Shatter these mirrors, shatter these mirrors,
I want to see the truest image of You.
Shatter these mirrors, shatter these mirrors,
No more reflection, but all that is You.

Here I am... take me, use me, send me,
Here I am... take me, use me, send me.

While attending the Isaiah 61 school at Singing Waters in the start of 2009 (yes, I can hear fellow students even now cheering uproariously). We were constantly being encouraged to listen for the voice of God, "tune to flow". I already knew I could hear from Father, what I needed to learn was how much I was truly hearing from Him and how much more He had for me to hear. I was learning that I had a prophetic gifting of poem writing. In a poetic form I was getting words for people that I would find out were right on and met them right where they were at. That was all fine; well one such inspiration came after lights out. Literally, I had just turned off my light for the night. All my writing stuff was not within reach, I was tired, but I was getting the words for a poem that I felt I was to write for a young lady on the school named Sian. Finally, I laid it out before Father that I was tired and that if this was truly of Him to remind me in the morning and I would write it. That taken care of I went to sleep.

The next morning at 6:45 am I was awakened with Father's voice as He asked, "So, you going to write it?" Upon asking what He was talking about, immediately the poetic words returned to me. So, I got up and wrote. Later I handed the poem to Sian and told her it was something I felt the Lord had me write for her. About mid-morning Sian came to me and thanked me for it as it was so awesome and right on. Then she shared how the evening before as she was going to bed she had prayed that she would like to receive a poem from one of the poetically inclined in the school. It was an answer to prayer, that God decided to use me for, so awesome.

Shining Star

You're a shining star feeling so far in space,
But you are located in a far better place.
You sparkle, spin and shine before the very throne,
A sheer delight for the Father's eyes alone.

But more than that you are truly a blessing,
With who you are, the Lord's glory you're expressing.
For shining star you are for everyone to see,
The manifest wonder of God's glory.

It's still a challenge as you learn and grow,
But dear star it's much easier if you let it all go.
Focus on just being there for the Father's Son,
For His bride, He's seen to the work being done.

Oh dear shining star, can you now see,
You can sparkle brighter because you are free.
The cares of the world are left behind you,
Just be His is all that you are needed to do.

So go on smile and roll your eyes,
Father's love in you, you can't disguise.
Yes, you are a bright and shining star,
One of Jesus favourite gems by far.

The Call of the North

In the land of snow and ice there's a call,
From a polar bear who is the Lord of all.
He stands to face both friend and foe,
He is the One who directs where winds blow.

He calls to you great hunter and your wife,
As you've learned His path into life.
Now stand as he does without fear,
He gives to you an unbreakable spear.

Go forth, go forth.

You have the sight, clear eyes of heart,
As two are one you'll go and impart.
Deep words of Father's healing love,
His words that are pouring down from above.

The spear you have will cut to the core,
Driving in a desire for more and more.
Stand in the north of long winter night,
You are His beacon of shining light.

Go forth, go forth.

While on a school at Singing Waters, I had the privilege of having my first meeting with a young couple who were Inuit. I got to experience firsthand how gracious and giving these people are from northern Quebec. Some of us were even blessed with watching how they craft their igloos. In response I wanted to bless them in some way and so I did something from my heart, the poem on the facing page.

I don't think I'll ever forget Bobby and his wife Sylvie and my hope is that our paths will one day cross again... on this side of glory.

Graduation Day

The bells of freedom are ringing,
Choruses of victory singing,
The triumph we've so longed for is come.

The halls of heaven stand open,
Corridors of the forgiven,
The freedoms we have not even imagined.

The throne stands there for us to behold,
The story has not yet been fully told,
There is so much more for us to come.

With faith we're willing to step out,
Trampling on past fears and doubt,
Heaven help the world, here we come!

The Spirit in joy will lead us on,
To the horizon and way beyond,
Bringing freedom to captive hearts.

The truth we know needs sharing,
In a land of the despairing,
The triumph we've so longed for is come.

It's Graduation Day!

My salute, to my friends that joined me on the adventure of Singing Waters' Isaiah 61 winter school at the start of 2009. May you have the faith and courage to see the words spoken over us as a whole and individually fulfilled. Each of you has made an indelible mark upon my heart which I can't imagine I'll ever forget.

I know that we all were impacted in some degree by the experience whether it be in class or otherwise. Take to heart and remember that Father had selected each of us individually to be a part of that time.

Like it says in the first few verses of Ecclesiastes 3 that the Lord has set times / seasons for everything. This is especially true for those who claim to be His children. Sometimes though we allow our circumstances to mire us down when a season of change is presented to us. Quite often it takes us a brave swallow and a step out in faith that our Father will be there to catch us.

Why is it that we like the comfort of same-ness and yet in us burns the desire for change. When will we realize that when it comes down to it, that when change comes within God's time table that there really isn't any risk, unless of course you don't want to be stretched for your own betterment.

It's Time

Rise up for your past is not your sum,
Rise for you are the total of what's to come.
The Father sees you for who you will be,
The time has come to take your destiny.
Release the roots of your past,
For those things will not last.

Stand up; oh man of God for now is the time,
Stand, for He won't accept any old line.
The Father calls forth for His son to rise,
The time's come, stop believing the lies.
You know all this deep within,
It's not been forgotten.

Stir up the embers of insatiable fire,
Stir again that inner burning desire.
The Father planted in you His high call,
The time has come for you to stand tall.
Heed the call of the Spirit's voice,
He waits as it's your choice.

Let the fear of God burn hotter,
See those chains will now shatter,
Grasp ahold the promise you know.
Allow the flames of God burn hotter,
Burn away all that doesn't matter,
I'm telling you it's time just let go.

Desperate Inspired Rant

The words that dance within my mind,
The words align in an array of verse.
The words that await to meet paper,
The words that long to come out of my mind.

The passion to express so many things,
The passion within both heart and soul.
The passion that wants to see pen ink flow,
The passion for there to be so much, much more.

Desire to go beyond to the real realm,
Desire to walk and breath and see in the spirit.
Desire to serve with complete sacrifice,
Desire to risk all that is myself.

To kill all that is merely fear of man,
To kill all that is me and not of Him.
To kill and let go of my identity,
To kill and arise born as a new creation.

Inspired by the Word of all creation,
Inspired by both music and by art.
Inspired by the words of precious friends of heart,
Inspired by words, passion, desire and the irony of
death.

Take My Life

In the quiet I hear Your voice,
Calling, calling.
When all alone I feel Your love,
Flowing, flowing.
Jesus, my Lord and King,
I give to You everything.

Take my life,
Refine it to Your desire.
Take my heart,
Purge it clean with Your fire.
I wish to be as clay within Your hand.

In the valley I know You're there,
Leading, leading.
On the mountain I see Your face,
Smiling, smiling.
Jesus, my source of grace,
I long for Your holy place.

Take my life,
Refine it to Your desire.
Take my heart,
Purge it clean with Your fire.
I wish to be as clay within Your hand.

Who Can Deny

Waters lapping upon the shore,
Washing waves forevermore.
Pattering rain falling down,
Hear the calm rejoicing sound.

Who can deny the Creator of this,
The shadow glimmer of Eden's bliss.

To the horizon goes the beach sand,
Realize the breathing living land.
The flowering plants reaching forth,
Creatures darting back and forth.

Why would one deny all of this,
The beauty of the Creator's kiss.

Rainbow arching across the sky,
It's not for you or me to try and deny.
This paradise in an azure sea,
More than a place, I unto flee.

How could any of this we deny,
Evidence in land, sea and sky.

Praises rise as if on sparrow's wings,
Listen as all of creation sings.
The voices are there to discern,
With these words I embrace my turn.
Who can deny the Creator of all this,
The hope promise of eternal bliss.

Here, I will confess what my closest friends already know. I love Barbados. I consider it like a second home, there's something about it that I cannot deny. There's a beauty to it that stirs me to the core. This poem was inspired while I was on holidays there in 2008 on a fresh morning after the evening of a light rain shower. From my room, I could hear the waves of the Caribbean washing the shore, the local birds singing to one another and the beginning stirrings of the resort staff and guests.

I know from personal experience that often it's one thing to just visit a place for a couple weeks and another thing to actually live in a place. However, I do often wonder what it would be like to head up a ministry retreat centre somewhere in the beautiful island nation.

When the World Sleeps

As the night breeze blows,
I hear a song rising,
In the dark streets it flows,
I hear someone praising,
Then I realize there's no one there,
It is nature's voice in the air.

> Chorus: Oh, when the world sleeps,
> And our soul the Lord keeps.
> Nature takes its turn in praise.
> When the noise is gone,
> Put away till the dawn.
> Nature's voice I hear in praise.

As the stars come out,
I sense a peace growing,
A soft, but loud shout,
A wave gently flowing,
And I desire to join the soft sound,
I'm no longer one who's hell bound.

> Chorus: Oh, when the world sleeps,
> And our soul the Lord keeps.
> Nature takes its turn in praise.
> When the noise is gone,
> Put away till the dawn.
> Nature's voice I hear in praise.

Bridge: The crickets and the breeze,
Sing for their Lord to please.
The shiny stars and birds,
Also know the words.
In this dream like praise,
My voice too, I raise.

As the song rises up,
I see God start crying,
The tears to fill my cup,
With a love undying,
Then I enter before His throne,
Where He beckons me as His own.

Truth In Nature

Lightning flash and thunder crash,
Bubbling brook and flowing stream.
Clapping trees and rolling hills,
There's more there than would seem.

Running herds and soaring bird,
Dashing dolphin, mystery deep.
Rushing wind, unchallenged breeze,
There is no secret in what they keep.

Searching heart and burning soul,
Deep within each man does know.
Creation speaks and creation sings,
His hand is everywhere you go.

Delving deep, so deep within,
Flashing gems and veins of gold.
Outer space, yet for us to see,
Those stars speak of the story so old.

Creation showing it to all,
No one who has sense can deny.
Darkness they try to run into,
They would rather believe in the lie.

Lightning flash and thunder crash,
Mankind will still behold the King.
Clapping trees and rolling hills,
In the end, His praise all will sing.

The Evidence

The clouds, the plumes of white that dance through the
skies,
High above, they sweep across the blue like a dream
flies.

The gilded sunset with its fingers on the water's skin,
Its final waves to the world as another eve will begin.

The brush strokes present that of the Master's hand.

The sky, the ebon canvas mapped out with gems of fire,
The silence, within its womb you can hear songs of a
choir.

The enfolds of fog and mist dance like they are a fairy,
While their dew drop children will linger and tarry.

The hand strokes, a shadow display of the Composer's
wand.

The east, the birth of day comes with the bright sunrise,
The caress of the new light is met by the starling's cries.

The day matures to lay the seeds of hope and promise,
The truth is there that not even the blind can miss.

With all these clues that point to the Creator's plan.

It begins like egg and sperm,
Hidden, but to the Father's eyes,
Like many cells that unite,
Letters start their DNA ties.

Down within the soul's safe womb,
Poem starts its life fetus small,
With subtle moves it makes way,
Heeding its own unique call.

The poet's pen starts to write,
Labour moves each stroke of his hand,
The timing set by its own clock,
Before long it sees a new land.

Then within this new big world,
Before all who would want to see,
The maturing comes to the lines,
Happy to live and just to be.

Here begins, change to this life,
Being like the endless blue sky,
The poet may be no more,
And yet Poem may never die.

Morning Prayer

As I wake to this new day,
Lord come and have Your way.
Even now before I open my eyes,
Father come and dispense all the lies.

Before I rise from this bed,
I surrender all that's in my head.
Even as my feet reach the floor,
You know what's beyond my door.

As I rise and start to dress,
My Lord, it's You I wish to bless.
Guide me in the world today,
Oh Father, come and have Your way.

Amen

Rainy Day

As I sit here with a favourite song in my head,
The rain patters on the window before me,
Capitulates a word that I contemplate,
But I conclude that it's not a word for me.

As I sit here with an array of thoughts in my head,
The rain continues to drum on the pane before me,
Desiring the time for poetry to flow again,
And low what is this composing before me!

O rainy day, your drabness is not within my head,
As you continue to tap the glass before me,
Promises from rainbows are what dwell there,
As I see beauty in the greyness before me.

The melancholy tune still plays on in my head,
As the rain cleanses all that is before me,
Completion to one thing that I've hungered,
This rainy day poem that is now before me.

Prayer of Boredom

Oh, Father deliver me as I sit,
As this moment is a boring bit,
Help me to grin and bear it.

Oh, Father help me to pass this moment of time,
Thank You for this gift of rhyme,
To survive the time that seems sublime.

Oh, Father lead me on from this place,
Thank You for Your surpassing grace,
And for the nicely timed change of pace.

Lamentation of a Cold

Oh my nose, my runny, runny nose,
It runs just like a leaky faucet.
To think this began with my throat,
Now I wish to hide in my closet.

Oh my head, my stuffy, stuffy head,
I almost feel that I just cannot cope.
As a cough escapes from my throat,
I grasp onto the tiniest hope.

Oh this cold, this lousy, lousy cold,
At least it's not a malarial ague.
As I reach for another cough drop,
I am happy that at least it's not the flu!

Cough, cough, cough, achoo!
Oh dear Lord, where's another tissue!

We all have different ways of dealing with colds and well, back on April 27/07 I was sick. I am not one who is easily taken by illness; I despise being sick (though I do like the cough drops). Anyway, on this particular day instead of getting down I was inspired to have a little fun. Now, I think it's probably one of my favourite poems to give me a chuckle.

No Nonsense God

I see walls of polka dots,
Closed doors that give up shots,
Pigs flying on high.
I hear fleas in circumstance,
Tied shoes in a real fast dance,
A mocking bird pie.

Chorus: But I, oh I, believe,
       Believe in a no nonsense God, a no nonsense God.
       No matter how strange,
       He will not change,
       A no nonsense God, a no nonsense God.

I walk down a backward street,
Feel the snows fiery heat,
Stars filling the sea.
I taste peace within the rage,
And freedom's kept in a cage,
Locks within a key.

Chorus:

I know of a servant King,
For whom the rocks will sing,
Songs filling sub space.
I see love devour pain,

In a land that children reign,
Time has no more place.

Chorus:

Bridge: One lamb dies,
    For a lion to rise.
    A kingdom upside down.
    Son of the east,
    West with the great beast,
    Do you know what's goin' down?

Irony; I don't know about anyone else, but I see it throughout God's creation. As fantastic as everything is, it's like He inserted these things that blow apart the box of theories that mankind tries to create. I still remember my first day in biology class in my Christian high school; the teacher said he had to give some time for evolution in the class. Then he said, "The bumble bee, proof that evolution does not exist. For by the rules set by evolution the bumble bee should not exist. There, I've taught on evolution now let's get on with learning about biology." However, even with all that there is, what it comes down to is that there's no nonsense with our Creator. Even when there is no sense from our aspect, He does have a purpose for everything that He does or allows to occur.

LaVergne, TN USA
15 January 2010
170026LV00001B

* 9 7 8 1 9 2 6 6 7 6 2 9 6 *